D1739196

Touch Of Heaven Collection

Where heartfelt poetry and the Word
of God come together to bring
meaning to those who need to be
inspired, comforted, or loved.

Leisa Spann

Touch of Heaven Collection: Where heartfelt poetry and the Word of God come together to bring meaning to those who need to be inspired, comforted, or loved.

LEISA SPANN
Website: LEISASPANN.COM
Email: leisaspann@yahoo.com

To:

Date:

Special Note Below:

Contents

Chapter 3. Hope, Encouragement, and Comfort

Chapter 4. Those Special to My Heart

Chapter 4. Those Special to My Heart, Cont'd

Chapter 5. Occupational Prayers

Chapter 6. The Sacrifice

Dedication

I dedicate this book to my Lord and Savior, Jesus Christ.

Years ago, before I had ever written a poem, I asked You if You would use me in this way, "Give me poetry and tell me how to go about using it to Glorify You, Lord!"

You have always been FAITHFUL to me through my obedience, and You have brought forth signs, miracles, and wonders.

For I am nothing without you, JESUS! Thank You, Lord, for ALL you have done in my life.

Prologue

Have you ever wondered if you were too old for God to use you in His kingdom?

The thought did cross my mind when I was thirty-five years old. Then I remembered that many in the Bible were a lot older than that, and God used them.

I accepted Jesus Christ as my Lord and Savior when I was fifteen. Being fifteen years old and a Christian in school wasn't cool, so I backslid. I found my way back to Him in my early twenties, but once again, I backslid.

When I was thirty-five years old, I knocked at death's back door twice within two months. I knew God had spared my life for a reason, and I was determined to find out why. I started going back to church and rededicated my life back to Jesus. I was on a mission to find out why, and for what reason I was still here.

A couple of years later, in August 1998, my grandfather passed away. That night I had gotten up at 3:00 am, with an overwhelming desire to write a poem about him. I knew NOTHING about how to write a poem except it should rhyme.

I quit school at the beginning of my 11th-grade year, and I had NEVER written a poem in my life, nor would I want to.

After I wrote the poem "Memories" for my grandfather, I read it back to myself and started crying. *Why did I wait until he passed away before I expressed my love for him?*

At that time, I felt a strong feeling that there was a need for poetry, for those that needed to be inspired, comforted, or loved. I asked God if He would use me in this way. To give me poetry and tell me how to use it to Glorify Him, and at the same time, touch the lives of others.

God started giving me poetry a few months after that encounter. A couple of years later, He started sending me signs, miracles, and wonders.

We can never be too old for God to use us. We just must be a willing vessel.

I have some stories about the poems I received because of my obedience and trusting God. Those stories are in my book, *"It's a God Thing!"*

Find the poem I wrote for my grandfather, on page 12. You can see the difference between what I wrote then and what God gave me, after becoming a willing vessel.

Memories

Looking back years ago,
as I was a little tot you know.

On one cool breezy fall day,
he was sitting way up there, on that picker so high,
I thought he could touch the sky.
He was on his way for a pick that day,
all I knew is that I wanted to play.

So, let's go have some fun
with a trailer filled with cotton you see,
that was fun for my cousins and me.

Papaw had a few hobbies too,
hunting and fishing was his cup of tea
he loved to do these things you see.

Never too cold even when
Jack Frost was nipping at his nose
and waiting cleverly for Mr. Buck,
no matter the cost.
I think one time he even got lost.

And if you were with him on that day,
you knew he always found his way
and ready to go back another day.

Papaw would get in the boat already,
hoping to catch some fish for that day,
catching a string of white perch, you say.

I went to visit on a spring day,
and the scent of King Edwards was well on its way.
All through the House, the smoke just lingered
and that cigar sitting between his fingers.

Now it's time to play the game, so pull out the board
and get out your marbles and your diced too.
I'm ready to beat you at Wahoo.

Papaw is tired he had a hard day,
time to rest his head, you all know he like his bed.
Now he's gone fast asleep, pray the Lord his soul to
keep..

Your Loving Granddaughter, Leisa

In the beginning God created
the heaven and the earth.
And the earth was
without form, and void;
and darkness was upon
the face of the deep.
And the Spirit of God moved
upon the face of the waters.
And God said, Let there be light:
and there was light.
And God saw the light,
that it was good:
and God divided the light
from the darkness.
And God called the light Day,
and the darkness he called Night.
And the evening and the morning
were the first day.
Genesis 1:1-5

Good Morning

"Good morning my love, it's a new day.

May peace, joy, and happiness come your way.

I hope you have a blessed day too.

Because I made it just for you."

-GOD

CHAPTER 1:

INSPIRATIONAL POETRY

Jesus said unto her,

I am the resurrection,

and the life:

he that believeth in me,

though he were dead,

yet shall he live:

John 11:25

Written In RED!

The words are black, and some are red,

this is how our soul is fed.

It gives us stories of water and wine,

with parables of fruit and vine.

We read of prophets, miracles, and a flood,

and the one who gave His blood.

It's told we can do all these things,

through one who's called the King of Kings.

The great I AM, is what He said,

all His Words are written in RED!

For this cause shall a man
leave his father and mother,
and shall be joined unto his wife,
and they two shall be one flesh.
Ephesians 5:31

A Wedding Prayer

As I come to you my Father,
in prayer once again.
Asking for a blessing,
for two becoming one
as their life begins.

I'm asking that you guide them
each and every day,
till death do they part,
as one they will stay.

And when they're having troubles
and they're feeling fear with doubt.
That both will call on you Lord,
and all three will work it out.

I pray you send an angel
that comes from up above,
to keep them safe in all their ways.
And they'll always be in love...

Consider the lilies how they grow:
they toil not, they spin not;
and yet I say unto you,
that Solomon in all his glory
was not arrayed like one of these.
Luke 12:27

Fleur-de-Lis

"Flower of the Lily"

This is the Fleur-de-Lis,
it's a legend of a special kind.
It's called the golden lily
that will take you back in time.
It's said that lilies sprung up,
from the tears shed by Eve.
Leaving Eden behind that day,
her broken heart did grieve.
It symbolized purity,
upon Christians back then.
For life, faith, and wisdom;
the old was new again.
It represents the Trinity,
the petals that you see.
The Father, Son, and Holy Spirit;
these are the three.
At the foot of the Cross
grown by Virgin Mary years ago,
a field of Golden Lilies
where her tears made them grow....

This poem was given to me by my trusting in God.
It has a story in my book, "It's a God Thing".

Purge me with hyssop,
and I shall be clean:
wash me, and I shall be
whiter than snow.
Psalms 51:7

Legend of the Snowflake

This is the legend of the snowflake,
it's like no other kind.
Each one is very special
and unique in its design.

They fall from the angel's wings,
as they dance before the Lord.
Singing praises to the king,
all in one accord.

It's the beauty of the snowflake,
a reminder from up above.
That I've been washed as white as snow,
all because of LOVE...

*This poem was given to me by my trusting in God.
It has a story in my book, "It's a God Thing".*

Let thy fountain be blessed:
and rejoice with
the wife of thy youth.
Proverbs 5:18

On Your Anniversary

As you remember days of the past,
your first kiss you fell in love.
In heaven the angels were playing their harps
and sprinkles of gold dust fell from above.

Two became one, till death do you part.
God brought you both together,
and put forever in your hearts.

Now you're at this day,
the years have passed you by,
God gave you both your wings,
you've taught each other to fly...

And, behold,
a woman in the city,
which was a sinner,
when she knew that Jesus
sat at meat in the Pharisee's house,
brought an alabaster box of ointment,
And stood at his feet behind him weeping,
and began to wash his feet
with tears, and did wipe them
with the hairs of her head,
and kissed his feet,
and anointed them with the ointment.
Luke 7:37-38

The Alabaster Box

This is a box that's a special kind.
It's holding something precious
that will take you back in time.

There she stood behind him,
with it broken in her hand.
No matter what the cost,
anointing the Master was her plan.

To her knees she fell,
with tears that washed His feet.
Wiping them with her hair
and a kiss that was complete.

So, anoint them in His name
and call out to the Master.
When you take this precious oil
from the box of alabaster...

*This poem was given to me by my trusting in God.
It has a story in my book, "It's a God Thing".*

Let them praise his name in the dance:
let them sing praises unto him
with the timbrel and harp.
Psalms 149:3

The Dance

When that day I stumble,
I'll think of 2 left feet.

What happened to my right,
doesn't mean to me defeat.

Sometimes I have to fall,
so the Lord can take control.

What once was a stumble,
is the dance inside my soul.

I am Alpha and Omega,
the beginning and the ending,
saith the Lord, which is,
and which was, and which is to come,
the Almighty.
Revelation 1:8

The Hourglass

From Alpha to Omega,
from beginning to end.
Does the hourglass of time turn again?

The Creator of one
and all that we see,
do we take that chance
or live for thee?

We may walk a mile
or a hundred it seems,
do we get the chance
to live our dreams?

What we take
or how much we give,
does this really reflect
on how long we live?

We never know
when it's our time to go,
so live each day like it's your last.
Because God's the one who
turns the hourglass.

Then spake Jesus again
unto them, saying,
I am the light of the world:
he that followeth me
shall not walk in darkness,
but shall have the light of life.
John 8:12

The Light of the World

Jesus Christ our Savior,
sent from God above.

Died on a cross,
that's how He showed His love.

He guides us through the darkness,
at any time of day.

His word's a lamp unto our feet,
that lights our every way....

Beloved, I wish above all things
that thou mayest prosper
and be in health,
even as thy soul prospereth.
3 John 1:2

The Locket

I give to you this locket,
with love that's opened wide.
I asked the Lord to bless you,
and be always at your side.

If one day you're lonely,
then look at this locket I gave.
Then you will know right then,
just exactly what I prayed.

I asked the Lord to send,
His angels from up above.
To surround you in His presence,
so, you can feel His love…

Now faith is the
substance of things hoped for,
the evidence of things not seen.
Hebrews 11:1

The Prayer Box

This is a prayer box,
that's a work of art.
Cast your cares upon the Lord,
it will hold what's in your heart.

He tells us not to worry,
and have faith as a mustard seed.
With God all things are possible
and in life you will succeed.

Prayers, dreams, and other things,
go in this box of love.
So, give it all to God,
and send it up above…

Above all, taking the shield of faith,
wherewith ye shall be able to
quench all the fiery darts of the wicked.
And take the helmet of salvation,
and the sword of the Spirit,
which is the word of God:
Ephesians 6:16-17

The Shield

May you be strong in the Lord,
and in the power of His might.

That you will take up your cross
against Satan and fight.

Putting on your whole armor,
and holding up the shield.

Placing all your faith in the Lord
and may you never yield.

Again, the kingdom of heaven
is like unto a merchant man,
seeking goodly pearls:
Who, when he had found
one pearl of great price,
went and sold all that he had,
and bought it.
Matthew 13:45-46

The Treasured Pearl

The sea can bring life or death,
and our tongue can do the same.
If we believe with all our heart,
as we call our Savior's Name.

The storms of life can knock us down,
which leaves us washed ashore.
What once was living in the sand,
beneath the ocean's floor.

At one time an empty shell held a living thing.
Just like the tomb of Jesus Christ,
that held our precious King.

So, if you see an empty shell,
there's a reason why.
To reveal the treasure once inside,
it certainly had to die...

And the angel said unto them,
Fear not: for, behold,
I bring you good tidings of great joy,
which shall be to all people.
For unto you is born this day
in the city of David a Savior,
which is Christ the Lord.
And this shall be a sign unto you;
Ye shall find the babe
wrapped in swaddling clothes,
lying in a manger.
And suddenly there was
with the angel a multitude
of the heavenly host praising God,
and saying,
Glory to God in the highest,
and on earth peace,
good will toward men.
Luke 2:10-14

A Christmas Blessing

As I shopped and went from here to there,
shopping for a gift to let you know that I care.
I looked and looked but I couldn't find,
just the right gift that I had in mind.

I wanted a gift to show you love,
like the blessing God sent from up above.
Something with meaning that's what Christmas brings,
a Savior from Heaven where angels sing.

I came to realize I'd never find,
such a beautiful gift of that kind.
I asked my Lord what should I do,
the greatest Christmas gift, Jesus, is you.

A Christmas Blessing is what I should pray,
for goodness and mercy to follow you each day.
And for peace, joy, and happiness with Christmas cheer,
to take you through the coming year.

Last but not least and most of all,
you'll be healthy and on you His favor will fall.
It's better to give than to receive,
so I'm giving you a Blessing this Christmas Eve.

CHAPTER 2:

BEREAVEMENT POETRY

Blessed are they that mourn:
for they shall be comforted.
Matthew 5:4

A Kiss

As we go through life not knowing,
living from day to day.
If good-byes that we hear,
are last words that we say.

And when we lose that loved one,
and we're filled with pain inside.
That's when our Lord and Savior,
is there to be our guide.

He sends to us His angels,
that come from up above.
In their wings they carry,
the one that's missed and loved.

There's something special for you,
to stop the tears from this.
And when you feel a gentle breeze,
it's your loved one with a Kiss.

So when you're feeling lonely
and need a Kiss today,
to feel a breeze upon your cheek,
a Kiss is what you pray.....

It shall blossom abundantly,
and rejoice even with joy and singing:
Isaiah 35:2

A Rose in Loving Memory

A rose in loving memory
that's written on the heart,
to show my love will never part.

The thorns are the pain that I carry inside;
like the dew drops on a rose
from the tears I've cried.

The petals feel like velvet
soft to the touch,
the memories are what I'll treasure so much.

One day the rose will bloom again,
when we see each other in Heaven, Amen…

This poem was given to me by my trusting in God.
It has a story in my book, "It's a God Thing".

Lo, children are an heritage of the LORD:
and the fruit of the womb is his reward.
Psalms 127:3

...but his mother kept all these sayings
in her heart.
Luke 2:51

A Son's Love

The day I left, I broke your heart,
you're crying tears from my depart.

I know you're hurting every day,
because goodbyes are hard to say.

I know you miss me,
because I miss you too,
but my love will see you through.

It's different now, not like before,
I'm in your heart forever more.

So, cry no more, we'll be together again,
from a Son's Love in Heaven, Amen.

In my Father's house are many mansions:
if it were not so, I would have told you.
I go to prepare a place for you.
John 14:2

Precious in the sight of the Lord
is the death of his saints.
Psalms 116:15

Sending Tears to Heaven
"An Everlasting Tribute to Your Loved One"

I'm sending with you a bottle,
that's filled with tears of love.
To take with you to heaven,
to that wonderful place above.

Please take it to the angels,
that are in the room of tears,
they'll pour them in my bottle,
where there these words appear.

"Oh how I Love You, and I will miss you very much.
I asked the Lord for you a Kiss,
gentle to the touch.

His arms wide open, for a Hug to embrace.
You'll hear Him say I Love You,
and even see His face.

All these things I too will miss
and you will never really know.
This bottle filled with tears of love,
not wanting to let you go."

And it came to pass,
that the beggar died,
and was carried by the angels
into Abraham's bosom:
Luke 16:22

The Wings of Love

The wings of an angel
come from God above,
and opened wide are wings of love.

The wings of an angel
to help us cope.
Bring peace, love, faith, and hope.

The wings of an angel
to comfort thee,
but God's sweet love is what we see.

In the Wings of an Angel far away,
is the one I love and miss today...

In my Father's house are many mansions:
if it were not so, I would have told you.
I go to prepare a place for you.
And if I go and prepare a place for you,
I will come again,
and receive you unto myself;
that where I am,
there ye may be also.
John 14:2-3

The Windows of Heaven

I'm going home to Heaven,
where there I'll wait for you.
Please don't worry about me,
because Jesus will see me through.

I'll see all the beauty,
and the glory that there is to see.
My loved ones who are there now,
are looking through the windows for me.

Hand and hand with Jesus,
we'll walk the streets of gold.
He'll take me to my mansion,
just like the Bible told.

All the angels that gather,
are there to welcome the new.
Looking through the windows of Heaven,
I'll be waiting there for you.

CHAPTER 3:

HOPE, ENCOURGEMENT, AND COMFORT POETRY

there for you....

Thou tellest my wanderings:
put thou my tears into thy bottle:
are they not in thy book?
When I cry unto thee,
then shall mine enemies turn back:
this I know;
for God is for me.
Psalms 56:8-9

Tears in a Bottle

Psalm 56:8

This bottle is a gift,
that's a work of art.
It will hold your tears of sadness
from your broken heart.

God sends to us His angels,
that come from up above.
They carry a golden bowl,
that catches tears of love.

They're taken back to Heaven,
to the room of tears
and poured into a bottle,
where there your name appears.

So, when your heart is hurting
and some tears have fallen too,
remember that Heaven's angels
have been surrounding you.

*This poem was given to me by my trusting in God.
It has a story in my book, "It's a God Thing".*

And even to your old age I am he;
and even to hoar hairs will I carry you:
I have made, and I will bear;
even I will carry,
and will deliver you.
Isaiah 46:4

Footprints in the Sand

Lord, I daydream we're walking together,
in the sand at Galilee.
You say I'll never be alone,
and your words will set me free.

I say you're my knight in shining armor,
fighting my battles each day.
You say you're my light and salvation,
guiding me every day.

Sometimes my body feels weary,
it's so much that I don't understand.
I pray your strength will carry me,
leaving only your footprints in the sand....

God is our refuge and strength,
a very present help in trouble.
Psalms 46:1

A Cancer Prayer

Lord, as I bend my knees in faith,
and bow my head in prayer.
I lift up to you someone
that needs your tender loving care.

They need the understanding.
Along with some hope too.
But really, it's your strength,
to see them make it through.

So, Lord, I ask this in your name,
no matter what the cost.
Please take this form of cancer,
and nail it to the cross...

And call upon me
in the day of trouble:
I will deliver thee,
and thou shalt glorify me.
Psalms 50:15

A Friend in Jesus

What a friend we have in Jesus.
He's with us every day,
waiting on the call
to walk right in to say,

"There's no need to worry,
I'm always in control,
trust with all your heart,
my word is good as gold.

I'm here to always comfort,
to wash away your fears.
My shoulder is here to lean on,
no need for all those tears.

So when you're feeling lonely,
down and out and blue.
I'm waiting on your call,
the need to talk to you…"

This is my commandment,
That ye love one another,
as I have loved you.
Greater love hath
no man than this,
that a man lay down
his life for his friends.
John 15:12-13

A Gift of Love

This is a special gift
that will mark the end or the start.
It's filled with lots of love,
that's written on the heart.

You can never unwrap it,
and the ribbon will always stay tied.
Place it in your book because,
the Cross will be your guide.

You will always know,
even though you couldn't see.
Just what was in this gift,
that I gave to you from me....

Beloved, I wish
above all things that thou
mayest prosper and be in health,
even as thy soul prospereth.
3 John 1:2

A Special Prayer

I Said a Prayer for You Today,
And I asked the Lord above.
To whisper into your ear,
that someone sends their love.

I didn't ask for material things,
for that's not important to me.
But I asked him to give you Faith,
for the things you wouldn't see.

I asked him to give you strength,
so you could endure anything.
And I asked for you a measure of hope,
for the Victory that this will bring.

This poem was given to me by my trusting in God.
It has a story in my book, "It's a God Thing".

Cast thy burden upon the Lord,
and He shall sustain thee:
Psalms 55:22

A Tear

Lord, as I lift up to you in prayer,
someone I love so dear.
My heart feels like it's breaking,
as I shed for them a tear.

Please take away their pain,
as you've seen all the tears they've cried.
And send from Heaven an angel,
with your love that's opened wide.

Comfort them my Lord,
because they don't understand.
How could this be, your will and perfect plan?

I want to ask you why,
but those words I'll never hear.
So, I'll stay on my knees,
and shed for them a tear...

Be not forgetful
to entertain strangers:
for thereby some
have entertained
angels unawares.
Hebrews 13:2

Angel Unaware

As I come to you my Father
in prayer once again,
I thank you for sending me,
my newfound friend.

I know it wasn't an accident,
no coincidence, or mistake.
It was in your plans that day,
a meeting in the make.

You knew I needed encouraging,
and lifted up in prayer.
So, waiting in your wings,
an angel unaware.

I made no call to heaven,
but one was on its way.
I thank you Lord for answering,
and sending her that day...

But they that wait upon the Lord
shall renew their strength;
they shall mount up with wings as eagles;
they shall run, and not be weary;
and they shall walk, and not faint.
Isaiah 40:31

My Faith

My Faith will stand
and my Hope will rise.

With wings I'll soar,
like the eagle flies.

I'll set my sights
upon the Lord,

my Strength and Joy
will be Restored!

Have not I commanded thee?
Be strong and of a good courage;
be not afraid,
neither be thou dismayed:
for the LORD thy God
is with thee
whithersoever thou goest. .
Joshua 1:9

Read My Heart Lord

I can feel my heart beating
without hearing a sound.
All these feelings and hurt inside
have me tied and bound.

Can you read my heart Lord,
and what's it saying to you?
I know you're only a heartbeat away,
and your love will see me through.

My body is weak from all the pain
I endure from day to day.
The darkness is as black as coal,
but strength is what I pray.

So, Lord, if you did read my heart
then you know all my fears,
and you've seen the hurt inside,
with all my fallen tears....

The angel of the Lord encampeth
round about them
that fear him,
and delivereth them.
Psalms 34:7

Surrounding Angels

The surrounding of angels that we can't see,
with wings of a dove, where could they be?

At our side, at work or play,
in our bed where we lay.

And when we pray to God above,
with fluttering wings, He sends His love.

To comfort and protect in our despair,
the surrounding of angels are already there...

So that from his body
were brought unto the sick
handkerchiefs or aprons,
and the diseases departed from them,
and the evil spirits went out of them.
Acts 19:12

The Handkerchief

This is something special
that will help along the way.
You were lifted up in prayer,
when I bowed my head today.

With every word I spoke,
it was in your despair.
I asked the Lord to surround you
in His loving care.

It will wipe away your tears,
if you feel you must cry.
I asked the Lord please let this be
His hand that wipes your eye...

The Lord is my light
and my salvation;
whom shall I fear?
The Lord is the
strength of my life;
of whom shall I be afraid?
Psalms 27:1

The Lighted Path

As you walk down the path
that God lays each day,
things will happen
that's thrown your way.

Setbacks, disappointments,
heartaches, and tears
are bound to happen
throughout the years.

Keep love, hope, and faith,
with God at your side,
and His light will shine
for He is your guide...

But they that wait upon the Lord
shall renew their strength;
they shall mount up
with wings as eagles;
they shall run,
and not be weary;
and they shall walk,
and not faint.
Isaiah 40:31

Upon the Wings

My wings feel like they're broken,
and my spirit can fly no more.
Give to me the strength O Lord,
so like an eagle I may soar.

Through the valleys
and over the mountains,
spread far and wide.

Flying upon the wings of the wind,
and over the sea I'll glide.
As I wait for you with hope,
my faith will be restored.

Because I now know,
I'm flying on the wings of the Lord...

Behold, God is my salvation;
I will trust, and not be afraid:
for the LORD JEHOVAH
is my strength and my song;
he also is become my salvation.
Therefore with joy shall
ye draw water out
of the wells of salvation.
And in that day shall
ye say,
Praise the LORD,
call upon his name,
declare his doings among the people,
make mention that his name is exalted.
Isaiah 12:2-4

Take My Hand

When I need your Strength, I'll call on you,
it's for the weary to help them through.

Your Love surrounds me day by day,
to feel your presence is what I Pray.

When the storms of life come at me strong,
I'll raise my hands and praise you in song.

And the Hope I have is to Trust your Will,
your words tell me to just be Still.

Lord take my hand and hold it tight,
My loving Savior my guiding light...

For he shall give his angels
charge over thee,
to keep thee in all thy ways.
They shall bear thee up in their hands,
lest thou dash thy foot against a stone.
Thou shalt tread upon the lion and adder:
the young lion and the dragon
shalt thou trample under feet.
Because he hath set his love upon me,
therefore will I deliver him:
I will set him on high,
because he hath known my name.
Psalms 91:11-14

Angel Kisses

Thank You Guardian Angel from up above,
sent to me through God's sweet love.

I know you're with me every day,
and your protection is what I pray.

I can't see you, this is true,
those Kisses from Heaven
were sent through you....

Blessed be God, even the
Father of our Lord Jesus Christ,
the Father of mercies,
and the God of all comfort;
Who comforteth us in all our tribulation,
that we may be able to
comfort them which are in any trouble,
by the comfort wherewith
we ourselves are comforted of God.
2 Corinthians 1:3-4

Tears of Salvation

Oh, hear me Lord,
as my heart longs for you.
You're my salvation, comforter,
and my friend too.

Sometimes I feel the darkness,
but I know you're always near.
It's truly my emotions,
that takes me down the road of fear.

You tell me not to worry,
and to cast my cares upon you.
But when I see uncertainty,
it's just simply hard to do.

So, I'll cry Tears of Salvation,
because that's the only way.
To feel your presence once again,
deliverance is what I pray...

CHAPTER 4:

THOSE SPECIAL TO MY HEART POETRY

A Friend loveth at all times,...
Proverbs 17:17

A Friend in Prayer

As I come to you my Father
in prayer once again,
asking for your help today
for my special friend.

I'm asking that you guide her
each and every day,
to give her strength and all she needs
to help along the way.

And when she's feeling lonely
and doesn't feel you care,
please put your arms around her
and let her know you're there.

I pray you send an angel
that comes from up above,
to keep her safe in all her ways
and let her know she's loved...

*This poem was given to me by my trusting in God.
It has a story in my book, "It's a God Thing".*

Children's children are the
crown of old men;...
Proverbs 17:6

A Grandpa in Prayer

As I come to you my Father
in prayer again today,
asking for something special
to be sent my Grandpa's way.

I'm asking for some sunshine,
that's bright and warming too.
That's how he makes me feel
as his love shines through.

Please send a little rain,
I guess you're wondering why?
So he will know how I feel,
each time I say goodbye.

Don't forget the gentle breeze
that feels like a kiss,
to always remind him
that he is loved like this.

For He shall give His angels
in charge over thee,
to keep thee in all thy ways.
Psalms 91:11

A Special Granddaughter

A granddaughter is someone special
who's a gift from God above.
Sent to a grandmother
to care for and to love.

Whose laughter fills my soul
that warms my heart, who holds the key.
Who brings joy and happiness to my life,
whenever she's with me.

You'll always be my sunshine,
and my angel that can't fly.
The love I hold deep inside,
that love will never die.

I thank my God
upon every remembrance of you,
Always in every prayer of mine for you
all making request with joy,
Philippians 1:3-4

An Angel is a Sister

An angel is a sister
who's sent from up above,
who comes to you from Heaven
a gift from God with love.

Whose smile is like the sun that shines,
that warms your heart you see.
God not only sent a sister.
He sent a friend for me.

I hold something so precious
its value is worth more than gold,
for this is the memories we share
it can't be bought or sold.

God made a wonderful sister
and He gave that dear sister to me,
you'll always be an angel,
my angel you'll always be.

For thou hast possessed my reins:
thou hast covered me
in my mother's womb.
I will praise thee;
for I am
fearfully and wonderfully made:
marvellous are thy works;
and that my soul
knoweth right well.
My substance was not hid from thee,
when I was made in secret,
and curiously wrought in the
lowest parts of the earth.
Psalms 139:13-15

Butterfly Kisses

"What are Butterfly Kisses?",
I asked God above.
He whispered into my ear,
it has to do with love.

At first, it's just a flutter
and then you'll feel it grow.
It's the Butterfly Kisses
that you'll come to know.

Nine months of waiting,
it's time for all to see.
The miracle God performed,
when He added to our Family Tree....

I thank my God
upon every remembrance of you,
Always in every prayer of mine for you
all making request with joy,
Philippians 1:3-4

My Baseball Player

Son, you're my baseball player
and I'm your number one fan.
You'll always be my little man.

No matter how old you become,
or how old I get.
I'll always remember
the first baseball you hit.

Run go run,
hoping you would get on base.
You should have seen
that big smile on my face.

When home plate you touch,
a score it will be.
After running those bases,
one, two, and three.

To see you play,
I'll hold dear to my heart.
Memories of you at the baseball park...

The Lord hath called me
from the womb;
from the bowels of my mother
hath he made mention
of my name.
Isaiah 49:1

Mother to Daughter

A daughter is a gift from God above,
sent to a mother to care for and love.

So did you know that your soul
is of my soul such a part,
that you fill every fiber
to the core of my heart.

Now you're all grown up
and a young lady too.
Yes, I've always been very proud of you.

In my eyes you'll always be,
my little angel, who I love so dearly.

Blessed is the man that
maketh the Lord his trust.
Psalms 40:4

My Heart Belongs to Daddy

My heart belongs to daddy,
who dwells within my heart,
for the unconditional love he gives,
from birth that's when it starts.

Through the years being good and bad,
remembering most,
my tears he wiped when I was sad.

For all the times he held me tight,
his arms of love, a Kiss good night.
God made a wonderful father
and a Daddy He gave to me.

In my heart is where,
your love will always be.

Keep me as the apple of the eye,
hide me under the shadow
of thy wings.
Psalms 17:8

A Special Grandson

A grandson is someone special
who's a gift from God above.
Sent to a grandmother
to care for and to love.

Whose laughter fills my soul
that warms my heart, who holds the key.
Who brings joy and happiness to my life,
whenever he's with me.

You'll always be my sunshine,
and the apple of my eye.
The love I hold deep inside,
that love will never die.

Who can find a virtuous woman?
For her price is far above rubies.
Proverbs 31:10

My Dearest Grandma

Grandma,
God decided years ago,
that an angel I shall see.
She wouldn't have the wings of a dove,
but full of love she'd be.

And her smile would be so bright,
that there would be a glow.
That is warming to my heart,
more than she would know.

Her arms of love would hug me,
and a kiss would follow too.
This angel that I see;
Grandma this is you...

Her children arise up,
and call her blessed;...
Proverbs 31:28

An Angel is a Mother

An angel is a mother,
who's always filled with love.
And has a smile of sunshine,
that's sent from God above.

Who's always there to catch you
whenever you take a fall,
and helps you with your troubles
and loves you through it all.

Angels have beautiful wings you see,
you know that really doesn't matter to me.

She may not have the wings of a dove,
but her arms that hug me really shows her love.

God made a wonderful mother
and He gave that dear mother to me.
You'll always be an angel,
my angel you'll always be.

This is my commandment,
That ye love
one another,
as I have loved you.
John 15:12

The Key to my Heart

As you look upon this key
and you wonder what I see.

That someone in my life
that God has given me.

You've unlocked something special
and God knew from the start.

That you would always have,
the key that's to my heart....

Before I formed thee
in the belly I knew thee;...
Jeremiah 1:5

Daughter to Mother

A woman has been chosen by God above,
to be given a daughter that's a gift of love.

He secretly knew she was a mother to be,
then whispered my name and created me.

My life was recorded from the very first day,
nine months of bonding was well on its way.

Our hearts are as one that's like no other,
me as your daughter and you as my mother.

Now, I'm all grown up still your little girl too,
Mother always remember,
your daughter loves you...

This is my commandment,
That ye love one another,
as I have loved you.
Greater love hath
no man than this,
that a man lay down
his life for his friends.
John 15:12-13

Footprints on the Heart

God sent that someone special
who walked right in one day,
and changed my life forever
leaving footprints there to stay.

When loving memories are shared
that walk upon the heart,
that God has brought together
that's how a friendship starts.

Every day that passes
the love just never ends,
leaving footprints on the heart
has made us best of friends.

So, every time you read this
know that you've been told,
your heart is full of love
and your footprints made of gold.

The Lord hath called me
from the womb;
from the bowels
of my mother
hath he made
mention of my name.
Isaiah 49:1

Mother to Son

A son is a gift from God above,
sent to a mother to care for and love.

So did you know that your soul
is of my soul such a part,
that you fill every fiber
to the core of my heart.

Now you're all grown up
and a young man too.
Yes, I've always been very proud of you.

In my eyes you'll always be,
my little boy, who I love so dearly.

Beareth all things,
believeth all things,
hopeth all things,
endureth all things.
1 Corinthians 13:7-8

Whispers

Your name whispers within my heart,
that's where you'll always be.
Like the whispers of the wind,
that's calling out to me.

The love that echoes silently,
embraces me each day.
You're like the wind beneath my wings,
that God has sent my way.

The love we share is always here,
it's been there from the start.
Because the whispers of your name,
will be forever in my heart...

And ye now therefore have sorrow:
but I will see you again,
and your heart shall rejoice,
and your joy no man taketh from you.
John 16:22

My Beloved Pet

Thank You Lord, for all the years
you've given me with my pet.
With walks, baths, and countless trips
we took to see the vet.

I gave back and belly rubs,
left always wanting more.
The love I feel in my heart,
fills every fiber to the core.

Oh, how I miss my friend,
so loyal and true,
has left me feeling lots of days,
down-and-out and blue.

The memories we share will always be there,
and will never go away.
Lord, please mend my broken heart,
the paw prints are here to stay....

CHAPTER 5:

OCCCUPATIONAL PRAYERS POETRY

Hast thou given
the horse strength?
Hast thou clothed his
neck with thunder?
Job 39:19

A Barrel Racer in Prayer

As I come to you my Lord,
on bended knees in prayer.
I lift up to you a barrel racer,
please keep her within your care.

I'm asking that you guide her,
around barrels one, two, and three.
Without knocking any over,
so there's no penalty.

Please give to her partner,
the strength to run the race.
A horse that runs like thunder
is sure to win first place.

So, Lord, ride with her today
and be always at her side.
A soldier of the cross,
on her horse for you she rides...

The Lord is my rock,
in whom I will trust;
My buckler,
and my horn of my salvation,
Psalms 18:2

A Bull Rider in Prayer

As I come to you my Lord,
on bended knees in prayer.
I lift up to you a bull rider,
please keep him within your care.

I'm asking for his protection,
since I'm his number one fan.
Lord, you know rodeo
is in the heart of this young man.

Riding a raging bull
weighing over a thousand pounds.
It's hard to stay on
until the eight second sounds.

With one hand holding on
and the other raised high.
He nods his head he's ready,
let's give this one a try.

Spinning and bucking,
jerking from side to side.
Sure, makes it hard for this cowboy to ride.

So, Lord, take the bull by the horns
and show him who's the boss.
Because where it started
was with you on the cross....

God whom we serve
is able to deliver us
from the burning
fiery furnace,...
Daniel 3:17

A Firefighter in Prayer

As I come to you my Lord,
in prayer again today,
asking for your help
to be sent a Fireman's way.

At a home, school, or business,
where the raging flames roar,
a hand that reaches out
as he passes through the door.

The heat is so intense,
clouds of darkness all around,
searching for survivors
that are waiting to be found.

I'm asking for protection
as he enters such a place,
your presence to be felt;
a hand to be embraced.

Lord, give to him the strength
and take and guide him through,
because the hand that he holds,
belongs to only you....

Follow me,
and I will make you
fishers of men.
Matthew 4:19

A Fisherman in Prayer

As I come to you my Lord,
on bended knees in prayer.
I lift up to you a fisherman,
please keep him within your care.

I'm asking that you guide him,
on the waters while in the boat.
Lord, he's a willing vessel,
that will always stay afloat.

And if he's having troubles
or danger comes that day.
Walk on the water,
and cast his fears away.

To find the fish for a catch,
he'll need to follow you.
So, you can show him where to go,
to catch a multitude.

My goodness, my fortress
and high tower,
my deliverer and my shield,
He in whom I trust.
Psalms 144:2

A Law Officer in Prayer

As I come to you my Lord,
in prayer for someone today.
Asking for your help,
to be sent an Officer's way.

I'm asking for the guidance,
with your wisdom too.
That he will know in all situations,
just what he needs to do.

Give to him the strength my Lord,
to protect and serve is his field.
You are the high tower, the fortress,
and the protector of the shield.

So, Lord, please be his partner,
and his back-up to see him through.
Because the one that he really serves,
is the one I'm talking to.

And whatsoever ye do,
do it heartily, as to the Lord,
and not unto men;
Knowing that of the Lord
ye shall receive
the reward of the inheritance:
for ye serve the Lord Christ.
Colossians 3:23-24

Lineman in Prayer

As I come to you Lord
on bended knees I pray,
asking for your protection
for a lineman today.

I'm asking for your wisdom
along with your strength too,
so the lineman can do his job
and carefully see it through.

And when he gets called out
hundreds of times,
your Mighty Hands lift him up
as the lineman climbs.

Please help him endure
all the rain, sleet or snow,
because those kinds of storms
keep him on the go.

As I come to a close
sending you my prayers,
God Bless the Lineman,
because I know he truly cares.....

He hath begun a
good work in you,...
Philippians 1:6

A Nurse's Prayer

Thank you,
Lord for your help today,
as I care for the patients
you send my way.

Let my smile
shine so bright,
to warm the hearts
of those in sight.

Please let my words
be kind and sweet,
for I don't know
the pain of those I meet.

And may my touch
bring comfort too,
for the work I do,
I do through you....

And he gave some, apostles;
and some, prophets;
and some, evangelists;
and some, pastors, and teachers;
For the perfecting of the saints,
for the work of the ministry,
for the edifying of
the body of Christ:
Ephesians 4:11-12

A Pastor in Prayer

Lord, as I lift up to you my Pastor,
on bended knees in prayer.
Send down your Holy Spirit,
to surround him in your care.

Give to him the strength,
to conquer what life may bring.
Neither faint nor weary,
for he shall mount up as eagles' wings.

Give to him the wisdom,
for it's your word that guides each day.
Lord, he's the one you've chosen,
to teach and show the way....

In all thy ways
acknowledge him,
and he shall
direct thy paths.
Proverbs 3:6

A Pipeliner in Prayer

As I come to you my Lord,
on bended knees in prayer.
I lift up to you my pipeliner,
please keep him within your care.

I'm asking that you guide him
each and every day.
Keep him safe as he works,
on the right-of-way.

Lord, plant his feet on solid ground,
so there's no shifting sand.
From pipeline to pipeline,
carry him in your hand.

And at the end of each day,
he'll owe his dues to you.
Because it was your hands,
that guided this pipeliner through...

Watch ye,
stand fast in the faith,
quit you like men,
be strong.
1 Corinthians 16:13

A Soldier in Prayer

As I come to you my Father,
on bended knees in prayer.
I lift up to you my soldier,
please keep him within your care.

Guide him through the darkness,
at any time of day.
Your words a lamp unto his feet,
that lights his every way.

Keep him strong and healthy,
for he fights to keep us free.
Lord, you're the rock he leans on,
and his strength does come from thee.

Send from Heaven your angels,
to protect him from any harm.
So, I can hold him once again,
in my loving arms...

I will instruct thee
and teach thee
in the way which
thou shalt go:
I will guide thee
with mine eye.
Psalms 32:8

A Teacher's Love

Teachers come and teachers go,
from kindergarten to college
they see us grow.

The knowledge we learn,
can never be bought.

This is something
the teachers have taught.

To teach is to touch the heart within,
a teacher's love is where it begins...

Remembering without ceasing
your work of faith,
and labor of love,
and patience of hope
in our Lord Jesus Christ,
in the sight of
God and our Father;
1 Thessalonians 1:3

Day Care

Come to the little children,
and love them with all your heart.
Teaching, cooking, and playing,
are all just a small part.

It takes a special person,
to love a child of another.
To do the things you do each day,
you're like their second mother.

Day in and day out,
a lot of hearts you touch.
A lot of tears you wipe,
and bobos you kiss are much.

You're a very special person,
to do the things you do.
Caring for little ones,
as your love shines through you....

CHAPTER 6:

THE SACRIFICE

Then the soldiers of the governor
took Jesus into the common hall,
and gathered unto him
the whole band of soldiers.
And they stripped him,
and put on him a scarlet robe.
And when they had platted
a crown of thorns,
they put it upon his head,
and a reed in his right hand:
and they bowed
the knee before him,
and mocked him, saying,
Hail, King of the Jews!
And they spit upon him,
and took the reed,
and smote him on the head.
Matthew 27:27-30

The Cross

Do you remember the cross
and how it came to be,
that God's only son, Jesus,
died on Calvary?

The stripes they put upon His back,
were not made of clothes.
But scars from strikes that day
were awful painful blows.

He wore upon His head
a crown not made of gold.
For His was made of thorns,
with cuts the blood just rolled.

The robe was purple in color,
gorgeous in every way.
The soldiers mocked and spit on Him,
oh, what a price to pay.

With nails in His hands and feet,
hanging from that tree.
We were on His mind that day,
He died for you and me.....

This poem was given to me by my trusting in God.
It has a story in my book, "It's a God Thing".

For by grace are ye
saved through faith;
and that not of yourselves:
it is the gift of God:
Ephesians 2:8

The Nail

He took the nails and died for me,
His body pierced onto a tree.

The Cross was carved from the wood,
and Calvary was where it stood.

He had no shame on that day,
that's where my sins were washed away.

It gives me hope and strength I need,
to have FAITH the size of a mustard seed.

That's where true love got its start,
that's when the NAIL became the HEART!

And they stripped him,
and put on him a scarlet robe.
And when they had
platted a crown of thorns,
they put it upon his head,
and a reed in his right hand:
and they bowed the
knee before him,
and mocked him,
saying, Hail, King of the Jews!

And they spit upon him,
and took the reed,
and smote him on the head.
And after that they had mocked him,
they took the robe off from him,
and put his own raiment on him,
and led him away to crucify him.
Matthew 27:28-31

Amazing Grace

Oh how He suffered on that dreadful day,
carrying our sins to the cross,
a debt we couldn't pay.

They wove the thorns into a crown,
to honor the king they said.
Placing a reed in His hand
and a crown of thorns upon His head.

They wrapped a robe around him,
spit and slapped His face.
Whipped and nailed Him to the cross,
that's Amazing Grace.

I wear my cross and crown of thorns,
to remind me the debt was paid.
For my sins have been forgiven,
where His love had been displayed.

For God so loved the world,
that he gave his only begotten Son,
that whosoever believeth in him
should not perish,
but have everlasting life.
John 3:16

Three Nails

They stretched Him out from side to side,
with His Loving Arms opened wide.

Two Nails were hammered into His hands,
and the Crucifixion was their plans.

The third Nail hammered into His feet,
with all three Nails were now in complete.

"It is Finished" is what He said,
to the world and bowed His head.

That day on Calvary on the tree,
He chose Three Nails and died for ME!

And they clothed him with purple,
and platted a crown of thorns,
and put it about his head,
And began to salute him,
Hail, King of the Jews!
Mark 15: 17-18

The Crown of Thorns

There was once a man that walked this land,
over two thousand years ago.
He died on a cross for all humanity,
for a debt He didn't owe.

He wore a crown upon His head,
made by the Roman Soldiers they say.
And they put a purple robe on him,
and chanted Hail to the King of Jews that day.

The thorns were as sharp as needles,
piercing through his skin.
They likely came from a date palm,
with long spikes that were not thin.

He once endured so much pain,
with all His suffering and shame.
The one who wore the Crown of Thorns that day,
Jesus Christ was His name....

And the angel said unto them,
Fear not: for, behold,
I bring you good tidings of great joy,
which shall be to all people.
For unto you is born this day
in the city of David
a Saviour, which is Christ the Lord.
And this shall be a sign unto you;
Ye shall find the babe
wrapped in swaddling clothes,
lying in a manger.
And suddenly there was
with the angel
a multitude of the heavenly host
praising God, and saying,
Glory to God in the highest,
and on earth peace,
good will toward men.
Luke 2:10-14

Come Let Us Adore Him

Looking back years ago,
a baby was to be born.
Only to find years later,
the mother would come to mourn.

Once wrapped in swaddling cloth,
holding Him so tight.
My Savior was born in Bethlehem,
in a manger on that night.

I celebrate my Savior's Birth
and call it Christmas Day.
I put up a tree with ornaments
and look for Santa's sleigh.

But what do I see within the Christmas Tree?
It's the Cross standing there,
looking back at me.

Come unto me, all ye that labour
and are heavy laden,
and I will give you rest.
Take my yoke upon you,
and learn of me;
for I am meek and lowly in heart:
and ye shall find
rest unto your souls.
For my yoke is easy,
and my burden is light.
Matthew 11:28-30

 *Goodnight*

"Goodnight my love, go dream tonight.

The stars in Heaven are shining bright.

Morning waits for you to rise,

you are precious in my eyes...."

-GOD

Special Thanks

First, thank you, Father God, for never giving up on me, and giving me this purpose to share with the world. Thank you for sending Your son, Jesus, who sacrificed His life for me, so I would have everlasting life with Him in Heaven.

Second, thank you, to my husband, Gary, who has supported me through this journey that God has laid out before me. I will always Love You!

Third, to my parents, Jerry and Nancy, my children, Nicole, Chelsi, and Canaan,
and my friends who stood beside me and loved me. I Love You!

Fourth, thank you, to my daughter-in-law, Victoria, for all the work you did putting this book together in Word. I Love You!

And fifth, thank you, Cindy Brumley, for all the long hours and hard work you did on the formatting of my poetry book and the design of my book cover.
You were a Godsend at His appointed time. May the Lord Bless you abundantly!

"It's a God Thing!"

To see what people are saying about this book, go to Amazon and insert the ISBN Number:
(ISBN: 9780999735657)
into the Search Bar for easy access.

"Amazing", "Anointed", "Up-Lifting",
"Miraculous", "Captivating",
"A MUST READ"

Made in the USA
Coppell, TX
09 February 2023

12496497R00096